I am a Hippo

Aaron Carr

AV² provides enriched content that supplements and complements this book. Weigl's AV² books strive to create inspired learning and engage young minds in a total learning experience.

Your AV² Media Enhanced books come alive with...

Audio
Listen to sections of the book read aloud.

Key Words
Study vocabulary, and complete a matching word activity.

Go to **www.av2books.com**, and enter this book's unique code.

Video
Watch informative video clips.

Quizzes
Test your knowledge.

BOOK CODE

E 2 0 8 5 0 5

Embedded Weblinks
Gain additional information for research.

Slide Show
View images and captions, and prepare a presentation.

AV² by Weigl brings you media enhanced books that support active learning.

Try This!
Complete activities and hands-on experiments.

... and much, much more!

Published by AV² by Weigl
350 5ᵗʰ Avenue, 59ᵗʰ Floor New York, NY 10118
Website: www.av2books.com www.weigl.com

Library of Congress Cataloging-in-Publication Data
Carr, Aaron.
 Hippo / Aaron Carr.
    pages cm. -- (I am)
 ISBN 978-1-62127-283-0 (hardcover : alkaline paper) -- ISBN 978-1-62127-289-2 (softcover : alkaline paper)
 1. Hippopotamidae--Juvenile literature. I. Title.
 QL737.U57C36 2013
 599.63'5--dc23

                          2012046232

Printed in the United States of America in North Mankato, Minnesota
1 2 3 4 5 6 7 8 9 0 17 16 15 14 13

032013
WEP300113

Senior Editor: Aaron Carr   Art Director: Terry Paulhus

Weigl acknowledges Getty Images as the primary image supplier for this title.

I am a Hippo

In this book, I will teach you about

- myself
- my food
- my home
- my family

and much more!

I am a hippo.

4

I spend up to 16 hours in the water each day.

I can close my nose
and ears to keep water out.

8

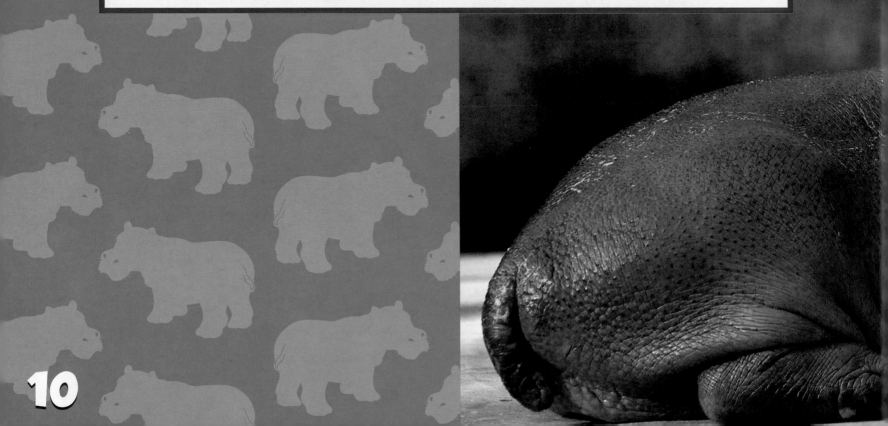

I have sticky pink sweat.
It keeps my skin
from getting too dry.

10

I have lips
that are 2 feet wide.

I can eat
80 pounds of grass
in one night.

I give birth to my baby under water. My baby can swim right away.

I live with other hippos in a group called a school. There are 15 hippos in my school.

I have teeth made of ivory.

I am a hippo.

HIPPO FACTS

These pages provide detailed information that expands on the interesting facts found in the book. They are intended to be used by adults as a learning support to help young readers round out their knowledge of each amazing animal featured in the *I Am* series.

Pages 4–5

I am a hippo. The hippopotamus, or hippo, is the third largest land animal in the world, behind only the elephant and the white rhino. Hippos average up to 5 feet (1.5 meters) tall, and 11.5 feet (3.5 m) in length. A full-grown hippo may weigh as much as 8,000 pounds (3,629 kilograms).

Pages 6–7

I spend up to 16 hours in the water each day. The name *hippopotamus* means "river horse" in ancient Greek. Hippos spend much of their day submerged in water to keep their bodies cool. Hippos are good swimmers, but their heavy bodies allow them to walk underwater.

Pages 8–9

I can close my nose and ears to keep water out. A hippo's eyes, ears, and nose are on the top of its head, allowing it to see, hear, and breathe while keeping the rest of its body underwater. When submerged, it can close its nose and ears. A hippo can hold its breath for five minutes.

Pages 10–11

I have sticky pink sweat. Hippo skin releases a pink, sticky oil that looks like blood. This is not actually sweat. It is a kind of natural sunblock that protects the hippo's skin from the Sun's rays. It also helps prevent the hippo's skin from drying and cracking, and even acts as an antibiotic.

Pages 12–13

I have lips that are 2 feet (0.6 m) wide. The hippo is known for its enormous mouth. Its wide, square mouth helps it grasp food. It can open its mouth 150 degrees wide. It will do so to feed and when it feels threatened. It will also open its mouth wide to let other animals, such as birds, clean its teeth.

Pages 14–15

I can eat 80 pounds (35 kg) of grass in one night. After spending the day in the water, hippos come out to search for food during the night. Hippos eat grass, but they will also eat leaves, herbs, and fruit. While searching for food, hippos may walk up to 6 miles (10 kilometers) in one night.

Pages 16–17

I give birth to my baby underwater. Hippo calves can weigh up to 100 pounds (45 kg) when they are born. They feed on their mother's milk. They can even drink milk while underwater. Hippo calves will sometimes climb onto their mother's back to get out of the water.

Pages 18–19

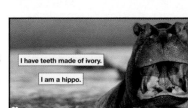

I live with other hippos in a group called a school. A group of hippos may be called a school, pod, herd, dale, or bloat. It can include up to 30 animals. Most of a school is made up of females, or cows, and their calves, as well as a single male, or bull, that controls the territory.

Pages 20–21

I have teeth made of ivory. Hippo teeth can be up to 12 inches (30 centimeters) long. Hippo ivory is valuable. Since the 1800s, hippo populations have declined steadily due to hunting. They are now extinct in many areas. Some kinds of hippos are considered critically endangered.

KEY WORDS

Research has shown that as much as 65 percent of all written material published in English is made up of 300 words. These 300 words cannot be taught using pictures or learned by sounding them out. They must be recognized by sight. This book contains 38 common sight words to help young readers improve their reading fluency and comprehension. This book also teaches young readers several important content words, such as proper nouns. These words are paired with pictures to aid in learning and improve understanding.

Page	Sight Words First Appearance
4	a, am, I
6	day, each, in, the, to, up, water
8	and, can, close, keep, my, out
10	from, have, it, too
12	are, feet, that
14	eat, night, of, one
16	away, give, right, under
18	group, live, other, school, there, with
20	made

Page	Content Words First Appearance
4	hippo
6	hours
8	ears, nose
10	skin, sweat
12	lips
14	grass, pounds
16	baby
20	ivory, teeth